HIPPO'S HICCUPS

Characters:

🟥 Hippo

🟪 Snake

🟫 Monkey

⬜ Elephant

🟦 Seal

🟩 Crocodile

Hippo: *HIC!* Oh no! I've got the hiccups! Snake, do you know how to get rid of *HIC!* the hiccups?

Snake: Try tying yourself in a knot. That always works for me.

(Hippo tries.)

Hippo: *HIC!* It didn't work! Monkey, do you know how to get rid of the hiccups?

Monkey: Try hanging by your legs. That always works for me.

(Hippo tries.)

Hippo: *HIC!* It didn't work! Elephant, do you know how to get rid of the hiccups?

Elephant: Try holding your breath
and counting to ten.
That always works for me.

(Hippo tries.)

Hippo: *HIC!* It didn't work! Seal, do you know how to get rid of the hiccups?

Seal: Try drinking some water and standing on your head. That always works for me.

(Hippo tries.)

Hippo: *HIC!* It didn't work!

(Hippo begins to sound nervous.)

C-c-c-Crocodile, do you know how to get rid of the hiccups?

Crocodile: Yes, but it's a secret. Come closer and I'll whisper it to you.

Hippo: Is that *HIC!* close enough?

Crocodile: No, come a bit closer so I can whisper in your ear.

Hippo: Am I close enough *HIC!* now?

Crocodile: Yes! Now you're close enough for me to catch you and eat you up!

Hippo: Help! Help!

Crocodile: Don't worry. I'm not really going to eat you! I just wanted to scare your hiccups away!

Hippo (excited): It worked — my hiccups have gone! Thank you!

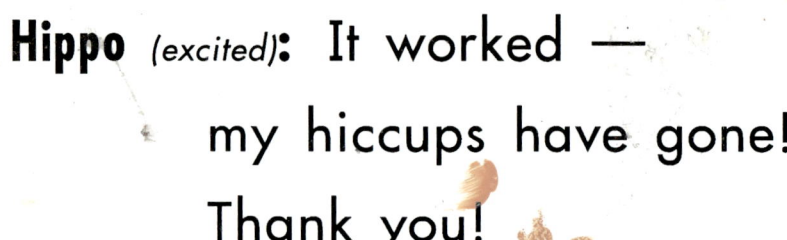